Y0-CPC-950

Praise for
For the Sake of the Children

"Every now and then you meet someone and you know immediately that you are in the presence of someone very unique and special. Roseanne Farano is such a person. She is a gifted human being who is blessed with unusual helping and healing instincts and powers. Roseanne lives the ethic and personifies the phrase 'unconditional positive regard.' People feel special when Roseanne talks to them, and they quickly gain a sense of optimism that she can and will help things in their lives get better.

Roseanne has been able to translate her voice, her message, her style, and her sense of humor into this valuable guide for divorced moms and dads. She has a way of identifying some pretty tough messages into series of simple lessons that have a single prevailing caveat: do what's best for the children.

I feel honored to offer my endorsement for Roseanne Farano and her newest book. For those of us who can't easily be in her presence, this is the next best bet. You will gain personal insights and will be uplifted by sharing Roseanne's healing messages."

—Dr. William Sherwood
Psychologist
Vice President for Human Resources
for the US fund of UNICEF

"With no exact English equivalent, the Russian word 'samochuvstvie' refers to the sum total of a person's pscho-physcial state of well-being. Roseanne Farano has become, to all those fortunate enough to know her and to have read her writings, the consummate caretaker of our collective 'samochuvstvie.' Her training as a psycho-therapist provides the necessary backbone of her clinical prowess. The essential element of her ability to heal and nurture us, however, is her innate intuition into the understanding of each of us and our individual hardships. Roseanne doesn't merely see through us, she probes and stops inside of us, with a compassionate desire to enter and share our experiences. She tenderly wraps her gifts of advice, wit, and spirituality and presents to us an enlightened path to where we desire to go in our lives."

—Joseph C. O'Connor
Board of Trustees,
St. Johns University

"With years of experience as a psychotherapist, Roseanne Farano has created a comical, common-sense guide for divorced parents raising children. Her quirky approach of humor and compassion is for all moms and dads struggling to talk to their kids amidst the difficulties of divorce."

—Annie Evans
Writer,
Sesame Street

"Roseanne Farano's work captures the spirit and touches the heart."

—Carol McCarroll
Ford Model

"Roseanne was given a gift—a gift that she shares with the rest of us. It's an ability to see and to understand beyond the point where the rest of us can't or won't see. In her presence, at first, you can feel like an open book, unable to hide the parts of yourself that you're ashamed of. But finally, to be honored by that sight and that understanding makes you feel lucky and happy to be human, to be the person enjoying the life you're living. Her gift is the gift of life. Roseanne is one of our great, natural wonders."

—Barry Alexander Brown
Filmmaker,
The War at Home

"With extraordinary insight, Roseanne Farano has us dancing right through the difficult challenges facing divorced parents today. Her heart and humanity go deep within, which allows right relationships to create new bridges of love and understanding. Everyone can gain peace of mind by reading her beautiful and humorous book."

—Maria Calegari
Ballerina,
New York City Ballet

Praise for
The Dove in Downward Flight

"Roseanne Farano has written a widely appealing, personal account of her experiences healing children. Her gift inspires the goodness and health-giving force that lies within each of us to be enlivened."

—Carly Simon
Singer-Songwriter and Author

"When we want to be moved by great music, we listen to a symphony. When we want to participate in making the music, we study with a master. And when we want to encounter the hauntingly powerful area of our own heart, we immerse ourselves in the harmonious mosaic of Roseanne Farano's *The Dove in Downward Flight*."

—Nancy Privett
Author,
Stepping into the Aquarian Age
and *The Scared Blueprint*

"Roseanne Farano has the gift of speaking deep spiritual truths in plain, easy-to-understand language. No fancy frills, just the plain honest-to-God truth. Goes right in where it's needed! Just read *The Dove in Downward Flight*, and you'll know what I mean!"

—Barbara Brennan

Author

Hands of Light

for the sake of the
children

ROSEANNE FARANO, M.S., ED.S.

THE OVERSIMPLIFIED UNDERSIZED PARENTING
GUIDE FOR DIVORCED MOMS AND DADS

for the sake of the
children

TATE PUBLISHING
AND ENTERPRISES, LLC

For the Sake of the Children
Copyright © 2011 by Roseanne Farano, MS, EdS. All rights reserved.

No part of this publication may be reproduced, stored in a retrieval system or transmitted in any way by any means, electronic, mechanical, photocopy, recording or otherwise without the prior permission of the author except as provided by USA copyright law.

This book is designed to provide accurate and authoritative information with regard to the subject matter covered. This information is given with the understanding that neither the author nor Tate Publishing, LLC is engaged in rendering legal, professional advice. Since the details of your situation are fact dependent, you should additionally seek the services of a competent professional.

The opinions expressed by the author are not necessarily those of Tate Publishing, LLC.

Published by Tate Publishing & Enterprises, LLC
127 E. Trade Center Terrace | Mustang, Oklahoma 73064 USA
1.888.361.9473 | www.tatepublishing.com

Tate Publishing is committed to excellence in the publishing industry. The company reflects the philosophy established by the founders, based on Psalm 68:11,
"The Lord gave the word and great was the company of those who published it."

Book design copyright © 2011 by Tate Publishing, LLC. All rights reserved.
Cover design by Kate Stearman
Interior design by Lindsay B. Behrens

Published in the United States of America

ISBN: 978-1-61346-850-0
Family & Relationships / Divorce & Separation
11.10.24

Table of Contents

Introduction

There was a very loud and insistent voice screaming so intrusively it kept me awake. The only way for me to find some peace was to get up and write down what the voice was saying. *For the Sake of the Children* is that voice, my voice, pleading with divorced moms and dads to see and hear what they are missing— their own children. My patients have been telling me their stories of divorce for over thirty years. This is what I've heard and what the children have taught me. Can you hear them now?

Nothing Beats Being There

Get joint custody!
Let me repeat myself,
Get joint custody!
Did you hear me?
Get joint custody!
There are *no*, or at least very few
excuses for not getting—
joint custody!
I don't care if you have to get up at five
o'clock in the morning for work—
GET JOINT CUSTODY!
I don't care if you have to travel to
Outer Mongolia for a living—
Get joint custody!
I don't care if you have to turn your life
upside down and inside out—
Get joint custody!

Any single mom or dad—in fact, anyone who
has a job—has the same problems, so—
Get joint custody!
Work it out, figure it out, even *get*
help, but get joint custody.
Trust me.
Your children will feel abandoned if you do not
Get joint custody!
No matter how much child support you pay,
No matter how many school events you attend,
No matter how many times you call—
Your children will feel like you
weren't there for them …
because you weren't!
Get joint custody!
Nothing, I repeat, *nothing*, makes up for
you, in person, alive and breathing, being
there; everyday, day in, day out:

For:
Loose teeth and first steps

For:
Cut fingers and broken hearts

For:
Burnt toast and missing buttons

For:
Lost toys and science projects

For:
Farts and burps and sneezes, giggles
and hiccups and bedtime stories

For:
Nightmares and dreams come true
You have to be there!
Showing up for special events just doesn't cut it!
Get joint custody!
No excuses, no justifications; you can do it.
Remember, you may have left
your spouse, but you ...
Do not want to leave your children.
So don't!

Get
joint custody!

P.S. There always seem to be exceptions to everything—so here are a few reasons to avoid getting joint custody:

1. Mental or physical illness

2. Abuse of any kind (physical, emotional, or sexual)

3. Alcoholism or drug addiction

Spiritual Insight: Just choose unity.

Chapter Recap: Be there.

He Said/She Said

Your children are not pawns.

Never,

never,

never,

I repeat, *never* pit your children against your ex-spouse. *Never.*

Get it?

Never ask your children to take sides.

Your children *do not care* who's right or who's wrong.

They just don't care!

Do not *use* (let me emphasize that), *do not use* your children to get back at your ex or as messengers or as pawns or prizes.

Just don't do that!

And, for goodness sake, *please, do not use* your children as your sounding board or confidant or shoulder to cry on.

Remember:

Your children are not your *friends.*
Go and play with someone else.
Get a friend your own age and
make them miserable!
However,
What your children *do want* is for you to *stop fighting.*
So stop it!
Get professional help if you and your ex can't work
things out on your own.
And if one or both of you is *so unreasonable* or (heaven
forbid) *so unstable* that you can't or just won't
shut up,
then, at least, take it *outside*!

Can I make this any clearer?

- *Do not fight* in front of your children.

- *Do not fight* about your children in front of
your children.

- *Do not fight* about "the divorce" in front of
your children.

- *Do not fight* about money in front of your
children.

- *Do not fight* about schedules, or holidays,
or car problems, or, or, or, in front of your
children.

Just don't do it!
And if you can't control yourself and you just have to
fight,
then
take it outside.

Now, this next one's a real doozie....

If you want to keep a secret from your ex, if you do
not want your ex to find out about your new lover,
how you spend your money, where you went last
summer, or what you do in your spare time, then
Do not *tell the kids!*
Do. Not.
I repeat: Do. Not.
Do! Not!
Do not ask your children to keep secrets from their
"other" parent.
Do not make them feel like they have *betrayed you* by
letting the cat out of the bag.
Do. Not. Put. Them. In. That. Position.
No one
gets to tell your children that they should not be free
and comfortable talking to

both parents,
about
anything, anytime,
ever.
No one ... Not even you!

(Except in the case of surprise parties.)

You really only betray yourself and your role of parent
when you burden your children with your secrets.
So,
Do. Not. Do. It!
Oh, and by the way—

It's okay, even important, to let your children know
that you and your ex are having difficulties (they
already know this anyway) but *reassure* them that ...

You and your ex made those problems so,

You and your ex will work them out.

If you and your ex can't work them out, I suggest (for
the second time) that you get professional help!
One or both of you obviously *needs it!*
Remember:
You got married.

You got pregnant.
You got divorced.

…

Your children did not, so *you* should work out your
issues.

What you should *not* do is become your
children's problem.

Whether you like it or not (and you won't), you and
your ex *have* to work together, even (heaven forbid)
attend your children's events *together:*

Birthdays
School plays
Baseball games
Teacher conferences
And oh my goodness yes, *even*
holidays.

You and your ex have to be on the same page regarding
discipline, curfews, homework, dating, diets, etc …

No matter how hard that is
and believe me it's
hard,
very hard,
Very, very, very hard.

So hard that you can start by just *considering* doing it, thinking it over, praying for patience, tolerance, understanding and compassion ...

but I warn *you*—

Don't ponder for so long that your children will have all grown up before you and your ex have! (Grown up, that is!)

As an aside—if your children are all grown up and you and your ex still have *not* (this means you're still either angry, holding grudges, and/or fighting), someone needs professional help (third mention), and I'm not talking about your kids.

P.S. Now for a brief word on parental alienation:

That's when one parent intentionally alienates the child from the other parent, either emotionally or physically.

This is done mostly by contaminating the child's view of the other parent through

emotionally charged,

biased

non-truths
designed to get the child to
dislike,
be afraid of,
or simply be disappointed in
the ex-spouse.
Don't do that … Don't do that
ever!

Spiritual Insight: Never—and I mean *never*—
blame anyone else for anything … ever.

Chapter Recap:

- Your children are not pawns.

- Don't pit your children against your ex.

- Do not use your children to "get back" at your ex.

- Do not alienate your children from your ex by asking them to keep your secrets.

- Do not alienate your children from your ex for *any* reason at all, ever.

- If you have to fight, take it outside.

- Work together to raise your children—actually be adults and parent them together.

The Truth, the Whole Truth, and Nothing But the Truth … Or Face the Consequences

Start by: *Stop* making excuses
                 (for the way things are).
                 Stop embellishing
                 (your side of the story).
                 Stop playing the *victim,*
                 the *martyr*,
                 the *hero*,
                 the *righteous one*,
                 the *sanctimonious one*, or
                 the *virtuous one.*
                 (Got it?)
Start by: *Telling the truth* (especially to yourself):
                 About yourself,
                 About the divorce,

About why you and your ex
can't work things out,
About what *you* are doing that
creates chaos and resists peace.

Start by: *Taking personal responsibility:*
For the marriage,
For the children,
For the divorce,
For the mess you've created,
For cleaning up the mess
you've created,
For your immature self.
Start telling the *whole* truth.
Not *your* truth
or
your *version* of the *truth*.

Try telling nothing but the actual, factual truth.
Stop weaving historic, emotionally-charged, embellished, one-sided (therefore lopsided), intentionally crafted versions of the truth, specially designed to make

you look good
and
your ex look bad!

Lopsided storytelling is simply a euphemism for lying.
It's
self-serving
and downright
narcissistic!
Besides, it really, really, really *damages* your children.
Really it does.

Bonus Feature:
Telling the truth raises self-esteem;
yours and your children's!
Say, "I'm sorry," when you are (even to your ex).
Say, "I made a mistake," when you did (even to your
ex).
Say, "I'll make things right," then *do.*
Say, "I need help," and get it.

Acknowledge your own faults and your ex's short-
comings (your children already know this about you
and them anyway),

without
embellishment
criticism
judgment

or
blame.
this takes some
containment skills,
will power,
practice,
and
an open heart... ...
or just some plain everyday
maturity!!!!!

- *Do Not* instigate discord or ramp up emotions.
- *Do Not* try to "get back" at your ex through embellished story-telling.
- *Do Not* try to get your children to "see things your way" or to "take your side."

Here's a *big hint* on how to know you are telling the truth:

The truth is never your truth.
The truth is a combination of all perspectives—
absent of emotion—
yours, theirs, and ours.

This is called the *Godview.*
It is all-inclusive.
And it's the only *point of view* that heals.

Spiritual Insight: When you wake up to a greater consciousness
(than your own limited point of view), miracles appear everywhere.

Chapter Recap:

- Tell the truth.

- Rely on facts, not emotions.

- Validate feelings (theirs, not yours).

- Validate reality (facts) without embellishment, bias, or storytelling.

- Do not enflame, criticize, condemn, or blame.

And (uh-oh, here's a big grown up word)...

- *Be responsible* for your own thoughts, actions, words, and deeds—it took two of you to make this mess—it is *not* just your ex's fault.

They May Be Tight,
But Walk a Mile In
Your Child's Shoes

Listen from, not just to, your child's perspective.
Their experience is very different from yours…
very different!

Put yourself in their place.
Help them describe it to you.
Don't tell them how *YOU* feel.
Ask them what it's like to *be* them.
Big tip: do not ask them to tell you how they feel.
Surprised?

Try it, watch your children's eyes glaze over, and see
how fast they close down and shut you out, with
short, curt, and inaccurate one-worders:
"Fine."
"No problem."

"Okay."
"All right."
"What?"

Do not ask them to tell you how they feel.

They either can't or won't tell you. They either don't *know* how they feel or they don't *want* "to feel" or they don't know how to *put how they feel into words* or they don't want to tell *you* how they feel.

Why?

Because *divorce hurts.*
Because *they don't want to hurt.*
Because *they are mad at you.*
Because *they are afraid to let you*
know they are mad at you.
Because *they are scared.*
Because *they are feeling emotionally drained, closed*
off, shut down, defensive, angry, hurt, sad, sad,
sad, isolated, confused, powerless, ashamed, and
guilty. (Did I mention angry and hurt, angry and
hurt, angry and hurt, and so very, very sad?)

And, oh yes, depressed.

Sometimes so depressed that they can't tell you how they feel.

Remember, actions speak louder than words.

Watch for signs of depression in your children, like when they are:

- too quiet

- sleeping too much

- alone too much

- losing interest in school, friends, sports, food, etc.

- shutting you out

- changing the way they dress and who they hang with

- dull-eyed or hyperactive

It's your job and your *responsibility* (there's that big, grown-up word again) to help them get to and release those feelings.

So what should you do?

Here are some suggestions:

1) Go to them.

Do you really expect them to *come to you* one fine sunny day and say, "Hey, Mom, Dad, got a sec? I'd like to talk to you about how angry I am at you and how much I hate this lousy divorce?"

"I'm a bit depressed and feel scared too. Oh, and by the way—could you both just get it together enough to take care of *MY* feelings?"

You need to go to them. You need to be the initiator.

2) Go to them again.

And make it easy for them, comfortable and casual. Ask them to *describe* their experiences, not answer your questions. Avoid asking questions with one-word answers i.e.: "How was school?" "Fine." Instead try saying, "Fill me in on your day." Then ask for details. Or ask them things like, "Did anything unusual or funny happen today? What was the best/worst moment of the day for you?" When they are being vague, prompt them with comments like, "Can you elaborate on that for me … I'm confused" or "I'm curious" or "I'm fascinated" (whichever response is genuine). Try simply showing interest by saying, "Go on, "Tell me more," "What else?" And please turn off the TV, put down the cell phone, stop texting, tweeting or otherwise telegraphing to your child that you have other or more important things on your mind. Give your child your full attention.

3) Go to them again and again and again.

They will try to convince you that they are okay. They are not.

They will act like you are a great annoyance to them, because you are.

You're getting a divorce for *goodness sake!* But don't let them convince you that they don't want you, because they do.

They will chastise you for "harping" on them.
They will call you a nag (if you're lucky)
or worse (if you're not).
You will hear choruses of,
"*Do we have to talk about this*? *Again?*"
Well actually, "Yes, *you do*."
"Why?"
Because, whether they realize it or not,
your children want *you*

to know what it feels like

to be

them.

They want to be understood.

They want to be seen.

They want to be heard.

They want to be validated.

And they want *you* to be the one who does all that.

And

while you do not need to agree with their perspective …

try walking a mile in their shoes before you decide

everything is all right.

Spiritual Insight: Everyone is unique. Everyone's experience is unique.

Chapter Recap

- Take a listen from your child's perspective (you have to, at least temporarily, be willing to give up your own perspective to be able to do this).

- *Go to them* … and make them feel safe and comfortable.

- See them … not just the situation.

- *Go first* … you be the initiator.

The Fault Line

No matter how many ways
and how many times
you tell your children
that the divorce was
"not your fault…"
they still feel bad.
They still have feelings…
feelings that won't just go away.
No matter what you tell them, you cannot tell them
not to feel what they are feeling.

Instead ask them to describe what it is like to be
them. Ask them for their perspective, their reality.
And help them talk about their feelings—even if you
don't like what they tell you…
Because what they feel is*:*
scared
hurt

angry

sad

confused

responsible

guilty

overwhelmed

powerless

ashamed

uncertain

cautious

and

just plain

bad.

Most of us so-called adults can't handle that much stuff—so how can you expect your children to be soothed by

"It's Not Your Fault."

"It's not your fault" is just not enough.

Help them out:

- *Go to them* (again).

- *Have a conversation, not a lecture.*
  If you are talking more than they are, you are talking too much and probably lecturing.

- *Do things together.*

Play ball, cook, hike, bike, swim, fish, build something, solve a problem, color, plant a garden, go shopping, etc.

Then let the conversations evolve naturally through stress-free time spent together.

It's simple:

You + Your Kids + An Activity = "a good thing"

- *Validate their feelings.*

    (Even if their *factual* accuracy is all screwed up.)

- *Separate fact from emotion.*

    Your children *will* have their *own* side of the story, *your* side of the story, and *your ex's* side of the story.

They will also have *feelings* about all three versions of the story.

Find out what those feelings are.

Help your children express those feelings even if you disagree with their version of the story, even if they have the facts wrong.

Validate their feelings *first.*

Then, and only then,

clarify things by giving them *only the facts;* not your
opinion, your point of view, or your side!!!
Be relentless. (One conversation
is definitely not enough.)
Be kind.
Be patient.
Be consistent.
Be honest.
And once they start talking …
Be quiet!

Spiritual Insight: Presence heals.

Chapter Recap

- Go to them.
- Do things together.
- Validate their feelings.
- Reassure them, "It's not their fault," over and over again.

Grow Up

Your children will gravitate to the most immature,
needy, unstable parent...
This is natural.
But
this is *not* good.
You are the so-called *grown-up*, so be one.

Try this:

- Stop living vicariously through your children. Get a life of your own, and friends of your own, and stop being "friends" with your children and your children's friends.

- Stop making everything about you.

- Drop the "*Poor me*," "*Woe is me*," "*Why me?*" routine.

- Stop complaining about the divorce, your ex, and how hard and unfair it all is.

- Don't try to "*buy*" your children's affections (more on this in Chapter Seven).
- Don't try to "*Out-do*" the other parent.
- Don't play the "*hero*" while making your ex the bad-one.
- Get professional help if you are depressed or can't control your anger.

And finally…
Either remarry your ex

or

move on.
It's time to:

Be Happy Now!

Your instability (whatever form it takes)
damages your children.
They *need* and they *want*
you to be
well and happy and balanced (so *you* can take care of *them*).
If you are not, they will try to make you *well and happy and balanced.*
Relieve them of this burden.

It does *not* belong to them.
It is all yours.
And besides, even if they try (to make you happy)
they will ultimately *fail!*
Don't set them up for failure.
You *grow up!*
You *take care of yourself!*
You *get yourself more balanced!*
You be happy!
You can. You really, really can.
Really, you can....
And
do it now.

For those of you who are already grown-up, try this:

- Get up every morning (well most days, or at least on school days) and make breakfast.

- Have dinner together *a lot.*

- Make *rules* and *keep them.*

- Set boundaries and *hold them*.

- Be *consistent, reliable,* and *dependable,* especially with your *rewards* and *punishments.*

- Be *realistic* and *flexible*. Every rule has exceptions, and every situation is unique...and yes, once in a blue moon there really are extenuating circumstances. Granted it's sometimes, not often; rarely, in fact, but there are an occasional few (even for teenagers).

- Let your children momentarily think they hate you (they will act like they do and they will say that they do, but they will get over it faster than you think...because what they are really feeling is their powerlessness).

Spiritual Insight: Reactive behavior is immature.

Chapter Recap

- Childish reactions are just that: *childish.*
- Childish behaviors inhibit your children's health and sense of well-being.
- Children should not raise children.
- Grow up; be *well* and *happy* and *balanced.*

You Can't Buy Love

(or self esteem for that matter).

Money really *can't* buy love.
Money is *never* the answer. It really *never ever is*.
Money really, really, really can't and really, really, really,
doesn't buy *love* (theirs) or self-esteem (yours)
or your children's favor.
It does not matter how much money you have
(or don't have),
You cannot afford to confuse love with money.
Buying your child the top-of-the-line
"I absolutely must have it right now or I will die"
designer outfit,
musical instrument,
baseball glove,
dance lessons,
summer camp,
prom gown,

skateboard,
over-the-top party.
iPod,
cell phone,
bobsled,
diamond necklace,
basketball,
swimming pool,
racehorse,
circus camp,
sports car,
trip to Transylvania,
Learjet (well you get the idea)
is insane!
Let them dream. Be supportive. Encourage their curiosity and explorations,
but
(even if you have money to burn)
you cannot afford to confuse
support *and* encouragement *for your children's dreams*
with your own
need-to-be-loved,
low-self-esteem driven
ridiculousness

Your children's excitement is contagious.

So

catch it

and

reflect it ...

But

It is *not* necessary to go broke over it!

Do you remember how excited your child got when
they first discovered their toes?

Remember how adorable you thought that was?

Well, *this is exactly the same thing!*

- Bask in their adorableness.

- Be in awe of their youthful exuberance.

- *Smile.*

- *Beam.*

- *Glow* with pride ...

But keep your money in your wallet

and

your wallet in your pocket.

Instead,

emanate happiness,

radiate contentment,

and

shower your children with the riches in your heart.

Yes,

Do pay for piano (or guitar or drum or trumpet or violin or clarinet) lessons, but don't immediately go out and buy an expensive, shiny new instrument. Until they are seriously dedicated or passionately musical, rent one, borrow one, or buy a pre-owned or less expensive one.

And

yes,

Do stop paying for lessons when they consistently miss them, stop practicing, or you find yourself trying to convince them that it's good for them.

And while you're at it remember that even though you may feel:

old-fashioned,

lame,

nerdy,

dumb,

un-cool,

and

totally dorked out ...

Teach your children the value of a dollar,
a hard day's work
and the self-respect that naturally follows.

Capiche!?!

Nothing…
There is *nothing* you can buy that will make up for
low self-esteem, shame, or guilt.
I'm talking about *yours,*
not your *kid's*

or

your ex's.
There is *nothing* you can buy that will convince your
child that you are a good mom or dad
(especially if you are not).
In fact there is *nothing* you can buy
that will convince *you* either.
But here's the best part:
Your children don't *need* convincing. They'll love you
no matter what
(even if you refuse to get them those $250 sneakers)!
Which reminds me:
You are *seriously* capable of creating a sense of
entitlement in your children.

Think carefully now...
Do you really want to do that!?!

So let's talk about child support.
No matter who pays whom, or who pays for what, child
support does not just mean money, money, money.
Child support means just *that*....
Support.
Support for your child:
emotional,
physical,
intellectual,
moral,
ethical,
and
loving.
(You knew that already, didn't you?)
Moms and dads need to be a part of a child's daily life
to provide that kind of support.
When too much emphasis is put on the financial
aspect of child support
the *best* part
of being a Mom or Dad
is
lost.

P.S. For those of you who are emotionally impaired or financially challenged, and therefore may not already know this:

Here's a definition of "*afford this*" for you:

- If the *cash* is not in your wallet, *you cannot afford it.*

- If the *bills* are not paid, *you cannot afford it.*

- If you have *debt, you cannot afford it.* If you have *no savings, you cannot afford it.* *

And finally
Beware!!!
Alert!! Warning!! Caution!!
Low self-esteem, narcissism, and emotional weakness have been known to masquerade as generosity…

So please, please, please, I beg you….
Do not confuse
genuine generosity
with
over-giving,
indulgence,
and/or

* Refer to Suze Orman's books for really, really smart and expert advice.

53

martyrdom.
True generosity only occurs when
the *heart is full*
and
it has absolutely nothing to do with the fullness of
your wallet.

Spiritual Insight: All human desires
are actually disguised forms
of our longing for
the light.
Be that light.

Chapter Recap

- Money can't buy self-esteem, love, or happiness, but showering your children with the riches in your heart and soul can.

- Child support means more than just money.

- Acknowledge your child's desires by encouraging their ability to *be happy now.*

- Presence heals; presents don't.

Let the Good Times Roll

Create a good life for yourself and your children.

Be happy, have fun …
But,
do not bring that fun home if it is wearing a skirt or
sporting a necktie
(and your children just happen to be in the house).
Your divorce has given your children more than
enough to deal with between visitation schedules,
adjusting to two different households, the two of you
"trying to work things out," not to mention the angst
of simply growing up.
They *do not need* your *histrionics* of dating.
Simply put:
Do not take your dates home.
And please, do I have to even say it?
No sleepovers
(while the kids are home)

and

living together—let's not even go there.

Introduce your children to your dates *only* when your children are ready and have adjusted to the divorce.

So

how do you know when they are ready?

Believe me; you'll know.

But if you don't,

they are not!

And as a last resort, at least ask them how they feel about your dating *before*

you surprise them with your new "friend."

And please, oh please, oh please …

Can you wait to bring a new person into their very upset, confused worlds for at least a *year* … please?

Go out. Have fun.

Just don't bring it home …

until that new person is a sure bet for a permanent place in your heart

and your children's lives.

Spiritual Insight: The purpose of life is to be happy. Happiness and pleasure are not the same thing.

Pleasure is transitory.
Happiness is not.

Chapter Recap

- Have fun—just don't bring it home.
- Give your children time to adjust to the divorce before bringing home your fun.

It's Never Over—
Never, Ever, Never

Your children will always be affected by your divorce.
It is part of their life … so
one great talk with your child is *just not enough*.
You must be open and willing to go over "the divorce"
again and again and again,
as their feelings
come up, evolve, morph, and mature.
You must be patient when your child asks the same
questions over and over again.
They want reassurance,
and
they want to feel safe …
So:

Make it Safe.
Listen a Lot.
Be Comforting.

Let them be hurt or angry.
Let them know you are interested
in their *point of view* (again), and....

- Let them know that their feelings matter.

- Clear up misconceptions, correct inaccuracies and untruths (with *facts only,* not with your *opinion*).

- Look directly into their eyes.

- Hold their hand.

- Be a dependable source of stability, humility, and consistency.

- Be reliable and responsible by *doing* what you say you'll do (your words should match your actions).

- Love them and express it.

- Bring up the divorce and their feelings about the divorce even, and especially, if they never ask you about it.

Oh, and by the way,
their feelings about being a child of divorce will
change as they grow up.

If you want a close and healthy relationship with your child, find out what those changes are!

Spiritual Insight: Obstacles
are really just opportunities.

Chapter Recap

- One great talk is not enough.

- Make it safe for your children to express their feelings over and over and over again.

- As they grow, your children's feelings and ability to understand the divorce will change. Be open to discussing their new perspectives.

You Matter ... A Lot

You are the parent.

It is *essential* that you actually *parent*.

Your words and actions, values and morals, *matter*.

So it is very important for you to:

- Be happy, grown-up, and emotionally stable.

- Be honest—don't cover up or excuse your mistakes. Be a model for your children by actually correcting your mistakes and apologizing for them.

- Raise the bar—for yourself first and then for your children. Never ask them to go first!!

- Walk your talk.

- Stop complaining—it doesn't just hurt your children, it hurts *you* too.

- Start being self-sufficient—it feels awesome and empowering.

- Be fearless *and* kind.
- Be understanding *and* strict.
- Be flexible *and* steady.
- Be conscious of. ...

And
never ever forget
The
unbelievably huge effect
you have on your children.
And
don't just love them ...

Love them enough to actually parent them. Be strong enough to make the tough decisions and hard choices that help shape their character. Guide them into being self-sufficient, empowered, compassionate, happy people.

And please, do not confuse loving them with giving them what they want.

Remember:

What your children really want is for you to:

- Provide boundaries—so they can feel safe.

- Be flexible—so they can grow.

- Be consistent—so they can experiment.

- Be stable—so they can find out who they are.

- But

mostly
what your children really, really,
really want is for you
to be happy.

P.S. Love is the easiest, most natural, abundant, endless force in the universe, so don't screw it up with any selfish, self-serving, narcissistic, ridiculous, and insecure stupid stuff!

Spiritual Insight: All characteristics you see in others are also in you.

Chapter Recap

- The effect you have on your children is

  Immeasurable,

  Profound,

  and

  Everlasting.

- You are very, very, very, important.

The Quiz

Here's a quick, self-explanatory little quiz to help you determine your true age—mature or immature (in case you don't already know it)—and to set you on your personal path to happiness (just in case you aren't already on it).

Directions:

Be honest.

No one will know how you answered but *you*!

However; *you* will know if you fudged the truth, lied, or made excuses to justify your answers.

But I warn you—
if you are *deeply, truly honest*,
you could actually get
some inner reflection,
self-awareness,
and/or

personal growth out of this!

And there's a *bonus* to this too ...

miraculousness happens when you are impeccably honest with yourself.

And finally,

let yourself be *amazed* at your ability (or inability) to be honest with and about yourself.

This quiz is self-scoring.

You'll know how well you did by the way you feel when you are done.

Remember:

Happiness is a choice,

not a condition, a gift, or someone else's responsibility.

Happiness is a choice.

It is often a difficult one, sometimes nearly impossible, but it is always there.

You can choose it or not.

I hope you do, as often as you can.

Good luck; Godspeed.

The Quiz

1. Can you apologize?
   Do you apologize?
   Is it easy and natural for you to apologize?

2. Do you admit your mistakes?
   Do you take responsibility for your mistakes?
   Do you work to correct your mistakes?

3. Do you blame your ex (or anyone else) for your unhappiness?
   Do you blame your ex to cover up for your own inadequacies?
   Do you blame your ex for anything at all?

4. Do you scream and yell instead of converse?
   Do you raise your voice to make your point?
   Do you shout more than you listen?

5. Do you "hang up" when you don't get your way?
   Do you need to be right?
   Do you need to win?
   Do you need to be "the hero," "the good-guy," or "the better parent"?

6. Do you complain a lot?
   Do you complain a lot?
   Do you complain a lot?

7. Are you often depressed?
   Are you often sad?
   Are you often hurt?
   Are you often angry?
   Are you often disappointed?
   Are you often frustrated?
   Are you often short-tempered?
   Are you often irrational?
   Are you often impossible to talk to or reason with?

8. Do you malign your ex behind their back?
   Do you pit your children against your ex?
   Do you use your children as your "best friend" or confident?
   Do you take great personal pleasure in making your ex the "bad" parent so you can feel good about yourself?

9. Do you lie to make yourself look better than you really are?
   Do you cheat or steal, then find a reason to justify it?
   Do you buy yourself or your children things you can't afford?

10. Can you be calm, cool, and collected in the face of adversity (if not for yourself, then at least for the sake of your children)?

Can you work together amicably with your ex (if not for yourself, then at least, for the sake of the children)?

Can you keep the discord between you and your ex away from the children (at least for the sake of the children)?

11. Do you need outer validation to feel good about yourself?

    Are you easily insulted, wounded, or feel victimized?

12. Are you the master of your own happiness?

Summary of Spiritual Insights

Choose unity.
Never blame anyone else for anything … ever.
When you wake up to a greater consciousness
miracles appear everywhere.
Everyone is unique. Everyone's experience is unique.
Presence heals.
Reactive behavior is immature.
All human desires are actually disguised forms of our
longing for the light. Be that light.
The purpose of life is to be happy.
Happiness and pleasure are not the same thing.
Pleasure is transitory.
Happiness is not.
Obstacles are really just opportunities.
All characteristics you see in others are also in you.

Summary of Chapter Recaps

NOTHING BEATS BEING THERE.

- Be there.

HE SAID/SHE SAID

- Your children are not pawns.

- Don't pit your children against your ex.

- Do not use your children to "get back" at your ex.

- Do not alienate your children from your ex by asking them to keep your secrets.

- Do not alienate your children from your ex for any reason at all, ever.

- If you have to fight—take it outside.

- Work together to raise your children— actually be adults and parent them together.

THE TRUTH, THE WHOLE TRUTH

- Tell the truth.

- Rely on facts, not emotions.

- Validate feelings (theirs, not yours).

- Validate reality (facts) without embellishment, bias, or storytelling.

- Do not enflame, criticize, condemn, or blame.

- Be responsible for your own thoughts, actions, words, and deeds. It took two of you to make this mess—it is not just your ex's fault.

WALK A MILE IN YOUR CHILD'S SHOES

- Take a listen from your child's perspective (you have to, at least temporarily, be willing to give up your own perspective to be able to do this).

- Go to them … and make them feel safe and comfortable.

- See them … not just the situation.

- Go first … you be the initiator.

THE FAULT LINE

- Go to them.

- Do things together.

- Validate their feelings.

- Reassure them, "It's not their fault," over and over again.

GROW UP

- Childish reactions are just that: childish.
- Childish behaviors inhibit your children's health and sense of well being.
- Children should not raise children.
- Grow up; be well and happy and balanced.

YOU CAN'T BUY LOVE

- Money can't buy self-esteem, love, or happiness, but showering your children with the riches in your heart and soul can.
- Child support means more than just money.
- Acknowledge your child's desires by encouraging their ability to be happy now.
- Presence heals; presents don't.

LET THE GOOD TIMES ROLL

- Have fun—just don't bring it home.
- Give your children time to adjust to the divorce before bringing home your fun.

IT'S NEVER OVER

- One great talk is not enough.

- Make it safe for your children to express their feelings over and over and over again.

- As they grow, your children's feelings and ability to understand the divorce will change.

- Be open to discussing their new perspectives.

YOU MATTER

- The effect you have on your children is immeasurable, profound, and ever-lasting.

- You are very, very, very, important.

About the Author

Roseanne Farano, MS, EdS, received degrees in counseling and personnel services from the State University of New York at Albany and holds certifications in Organizational Development, Executive Techniques, Investment in Excellence, Interaction Management, Energy Psychodynamics, and Hypnotherapy. Formerly holding positions as a college professor, corporate executive in human resource management development and training, and the dean of a major nontraditional school, Farano has also maintained a private psychotherapy practice for more than thirty years. She is a widely renowned inspirational speaker and teacher on the subjects of psychodynamics, interpersonal relationships, and the power of personal awareness. She has a unique way of leading people into self-revelation by exposing our predilection to seek answers from external sources rather than recognize that the path to happiness leads inward.

Farano's first book, *The Dove in Downward Flight*, was critically acclaimed, receiving four stars and an "exceptional read" rating from *Today's Books*.

To contact Roseanne about speaking engagements, interviews, or appearances, please call 239–642–8009 or e-mail Roseanne at thedidf@gmail.com. To schedule a private session with Roseanne call 239–642–8009.

Other Books by Roseanne Farano

The Dove in Downward Flight